# Dr. Beth Leigh

# Quality woman

*How to be a good wife and mother*

*Dedicated*

*To my sweet parents Mr and Mrs Benjamin*

*And to my big daddy and mummy Rev. Dr. &Mrs. Vincent.*

*And also to my siblings ,teachers and well wishers for their words of*

*encouragement.*

# Contents



*1.*

*2.*

*3.*

*4.*

*5.*

*6.*

*7.*

*8.*

*9.*

*10.*

*11.*

*12.*

# Foreword

For all wives and mothers, learning to love your partner and children should be your major concern and priority.what does love entails? what are your plans for putting it into action? if you want a happy marriage and a happy home,you must ensure that you are doing your part.This book is writen for ladies who are trying to figure out how to be decent wives and mothers.Most women ,have never been taught how to be decent and quality partners.they dont have positive examples of how to be a quality woman while growing up. As a result,they enter adulthood without knowing how to be a quality wife and                                                   mum.

# Acknowledgement

To GOD ALMIGHTY for making my write-up possible,May His name be forever praised.

# 1

# QUALITY WOMAN 1

A GOOD WIFE

Quality woman is a woman with good qualities.

Every man looks for a perfect woman even though the exact things they want in a woman vary. But a common theme is to find someone who is willing to ride the rollercoaster of life with them and who will stand by them in all situations. That is why they take time to commit.

Finding 'the one' is a crucial decision men make in life. They put in a lot of thought. They are not only looking for a decent woman who can help them, share responsibilities, and support them when they are down but also a woman who is free-spirited, experimental, ambitious, takes care of her body, and expresses her needs and wants. Many things go into making a man decide which woman they want to settle down with. Here is a list of qualities that men look for in a woman with whom they want to spend their life.

1. Honest and Trustworthy

Trust is critical to a healthy relationship, so this one shouldn't come as a surprise.

You want to be able to trust your partner to tell you the truth —
especially when it matters most. You want to be able to take them at
their word when they promise you something.

qualities of a good woman
This quality is not something you can afford to take for granted.

## 2. Authentic or Genuine

An authentic person has a much stronger sense of self than a
social chameleon who changes their outward behavior to fit in with a
group or to work a room.

We all adapt to different situations to some extent, but the authentic
person remains essentially who they are. You can trust that when
you meet them, the personality you experience will be theirs — not
just one they're trying on to make a good impression.

## 3. Independent and Self-Reliant

Your life partner should be someone who isn't afraid to be alone
or self-reliant. Even if their work doesn't yet generate enough
income to support them, you can see them putting in the work every
day to build something with growth potential.

Their independence makes them unwilling to make the load on your shoulders any heavier than it needs to be. Your lot shouldn't be any harder on their account. If anything, they'll do what they can to make life better for both of you.

4. Intelligent and Curious

You want someone you can talk to about things that matter to you. And when you hear them speak animatedly on the things that matter to them, you want to feel a connection and a real interest in what they're saying.

Intelligence is about more than whether or not they finished school or went to college. You see it more in someone's mindset, their words, and in the actions they take than in a piece of paper or the results of an IQ test.

5. Self-Confident

When someone is confident, they don't need you to tell them they deserve to be treated with kindness and respect. They know their value, and they make it a priority to put their admirable qualities to good use.

qualities of a good woman

They don't waste time or oxygen on false humility or pointless self-deprecation. They know they're awesome, and they're not afraid to show it or to make the big ask. They know they're worth it.

## 6. Supportive

Like anyone else, you want a partner who will support your goals and celebrate your successes with you. They won't try to steal the spotlight, nor will they ever make light of what you've accomplished.

And if you stumble, they'll be there to help you back onto your feet. They'll also expect the same of you. It's a mutual stepping up. Neither of you leaves the other to flounder.

## 7. Empathetic

The best listeners know how to empathize with the person to whom they're listening. They can put themselves in your shoes and, at least to some extent, feel what you're feeling, which helps them understand your perspective.

## 8. Compassionate and Forgiving

Empathy helps with compassion, but the latter is nothing without meaningful words or action. Without compassion, it's more challenging to forgive someone who's hurt you, even when they apologize and do what they can to make amends.

qualities of a good woman

You want someone who accepts and loves you just as you are and who will forgive you when you screw up and apologize for the hurt you've caused.

## 9. Kind and Thoughtful

Real kindness isn't something reserved for an elite few. You want a partner who is as kind to a grocery store employee or a waitperson as she is to her boss or you.

The good woman is human, so maybe sometimes she's less patient than at other times, but she does her best to be kind to everyone, whatever their job or background. Because their situation could just as easily be hers. And being decent to others costs her nothing.

## 10. Willing to Meet You Halfway

She won't sacrifice her most cherished values to make you or anyone else happy. But if she can make a compromise that doesn't violate her personal code, she will, as long as what comes of it is better than the result of not compromising.

If it costs you both something to make that compromise, she'll weigh the pros and cons and do what she can to honor your values as well as her own.

## 11. Consistent and Reliable

You want someone who's more or less consistent in her behavior because you want to know you can depend on her.

qualities of a good woman

If she's on a non-stop roller coaster ride and keeps you guessing as to how she'll act the next time you see her, the relationship will never feel stable or solid.

## 12. Classy and Charming

You're looking for a woman with class, which is not the same as expensive taste or snobbishness. A classy woman can transform a room with minimal expense. She brightens up every space she enters with a genuine smile, effortless charm, and natural poise.

She puts you and others at ease, making you feel on top of the world when you're together. Everything about her feels refreshing, and she leaves people feeling better than before.

## 13. Playful and Humorous

Your life partner should have a lively sense of humor and a tireless appreciation for laughter and fun. She has a thousand and one ideas for lifting your spirits when you're feeling low, but she won't use them to overwhelm or pressure you.

She seems to know just when to draw you out of your head and into something you can both enjoy.

## 14. Inspiring

She challenges you to keep learning and growing, even when you're tempted to wonder why anyone bothers. Just being around her makes you want to be better and to do more.

She gets you (better than anyone else does), so she doesn't nag or use passive aggression to pressure you into doing something. She doesn't have to.

Just watching her makes you proud and inspires you to level up.

15. Down-to-Earth

This good woman you seek knows you're both living in the real world with real problems. So, she keeps her head clear and her hands ready. She doesn't wait for a fixer to come along and make her life easier. She rolls up her sleeves and gets it done. .

She laughs and cries with others without embarrassment, and she'll always, *always* be there for you. She gratefully accepts every joy and doesn't ask to be spared the pain that often goes with it.

## 16. Passionate

You want to see your partner's face light up when she's involved in something she's passionate about. You want that for everyone, of course, but when you watch her, it's hard not to share the passion she feels.

It's also hard not to be reminded of your own passion projects and to wonder where they could lead.

*17. Open to Learning*

She's always learning. If anyone can make the absolute best of every natural gift and learned skill, it's she. You've never met someone more curious about so many different things.

While she knows how to kick back with some light reading or a fun movie, it's not long before, once again, she's immersed in learning something                                    new.

# 2

# QUALITY WOMAN 11

A GOOD MOTHER

Qualities Of A Good Mother

1_Be A Good Role Model

You are the first person your child ever knows. They've been with you right from when their little life was created.

As such, you are the first role model they have ever known. It's important to be an exemplary role model for your children.

Kids copy and learn everything from their parents as they are growing up.

If you want them to say please and thank you, tidy up after themselves, or help others – then you need to do these things too.

Show them how they should behave, be the role model your children need you to be.

You can't expect your child to do these things if you aren't willing to them yourself.

How To Be A Good Mother

2 – Set Boundaries And Rules

Children need boundaries to thrive. They need to know what they can and can't do and when.

Therefore, it's important to set clear boundaries so that they know what to expect.

You should always be consistent with these rules too.

It's no good changing them all the time. Your child will become confused as to what is expected of them.

The same is also true for when you have to discipline them.

The punishments need to be consistent, it's no good one time not disciplining them for breaking a rule and the next time not.

You will send them mixed messages.

The punishment should fit the crime. Don't give out a big punishment for a simple breaking of the rules – keep those for when they properly step out of line.

How To Be A Good Mother

3 – Be Respectful

Respect is two sided. If you want your child to show you respect, you also need to show and give them respect in return.

It doesn't matter that they are much younger than you, or that you're the adult. Respect should always be given. Remember what I said about being a wonderful role model earlier?

# 3

# SKILLS OF A GOOD MOTHER

What Are The Skills Of A Good Mother?

In order to qualify as a good mother, one has to develop certain parenting skills. These are the skills that make a good mother:

1. Positive Reinforcement

A good mother will not only spend time with her kids to ensure that they do well at school and in other aspects of life but she will also acknowledge all the right things they have done by encouraging them, complimenting them, praising them whenever necessary.

2. Social Skill

Social skills are developed by spending time with other people. A good mother will arrange her child's social life, take him/her to play dates and parties, enrol in school activities where the kid can interact with many different children his age.

3. Life Skills

There is no better mentor than a loving parent who teaches his/her child the basics of life, from basic financial management to the value of hard work.


4. Positive Behaviours

A good mother will try to learn from her own mistakes in the past and those she has seen other people make. She will use that knowledge to guide her child in making good decisions, showing him/her what is right and what is wrong, teaching him/her how to bring up his/her values in a positive way.

# 4

# RESPONSIBILITY OF A GOOD MOTHER

What Are The Responsibilities Of A Good Mother?

Being a mother is one of the most important jobs in the world. Mothers are responsible for teaching their children how to be caring, respectful and empathetic adults. The following list highlights the top 10 responsibilities of a mother :

Teach your child about gender equality and respect

Encourage independence from an early age

Help your child build self esteem by complimenting them often on their accomplishments

Ensure your child values their body and the bodies of others by

Teach your child to take care of their body and mind by providing nutritious food, getting enough sleep, staying active and learning life skills like cooking

Discuss how bad behaviour is not acceptable

Teach empathy for others by showing how to be kind and understanding

Help your child to have a positive attitude towards their education

Help teach communication skills and manners. For example: teaching the importance of saying "please" or "thank you."

Teach them to take care of their belongings by putting away toys, picking up dirty laundry, tidying up bedroom etc

# 5

# CHARACTERISTICS OF A GOOD MOTHER

What Are The Characteristics Of A Good Mother?

I've been thinking long and hard about what qualities make a good mum and what is the main characteristic of a mother.

However, in the end I've decided this is too big a question for one mum/me to answer.

There are so many outlooks on being a mum. So I wanted to get a variety of responses from lots of different mums.

So I have asked some of my great blogging mummy friends what they thought too.

1_I Am River – I think the most important quality a mum can have is just believing in your children no matter what. I have two sons, the youngest has Down Syndrome, but I genuinely believe they will both achieve great things. Support and belief. The material stuff is just decoration.

2_My Boys Club – Always trying your best as a parent – no one can be the best at everything – and not only doing it yourself but also helping your children understand that.

3_Family Travel With Ellie – A good mum is one whose children can go to them at anytime and talk to them about anything with no fear of being judged. They know you will love and help them with whatever life throws at them.

4_The Money Whisperer – Listening is high up there. By always listening to a little person, we encourage them to talk to us whether it's something good or bad, and we give them the skills to be a good listener themselves.

5_Mummy Cat Notes – One quality I feel that is important is trusting and believing your children, they need to know that while you can be tough; you have their side with everything, my son recently dealt with a bully at school (who pointed the blame at my son and his friend) and it took awhile for him to actually open up and tell me and I made it clear to him that he can trust me and that I was there for him and more importantly that I understand

6_ Emma Reed – To be able to be there for your child no matter what and to provide them with a loving environment to grow up in

7_Hello Little Lovely – Unconditional love and forgiveness. I think you need to give children a lot of grace in order for them to understand how to extend it to others.

8_Five Little Doves – Honesty. I am very honest with my children about the mistakes I have made, but I explain to them the reasons I made them and the regrets I have, I hope it prevents them from making the same mistakes as they grow.

<u>9.  Lylia Rose</u> – Having oodles of patience definitely helps!

10 –Mighty mama bear _Instilling the belief in children that they can achieve anything if they put their mind to it and encouraging them to dream. I think it's so important that they have that self belief in a world of doubters and nay-sayers.

# 6

# TRAITS OF A GODLY WIFE AND MOTHER

Six Traits of a Godly Wife

1) A Godly Woman Always Seeks to be Modest in Her Dress. Then out came a woman to meet him, dressed like a prostitute and with crafty intent. (NIV). (Proverbs 7:10)

By contrast, the ungodly woman's clothing points to herself and her body instead of her Father in Heaven and His holiness. Remember the words of Paul in the New Testament? God emphasizes a beauty of the unseen character. The flesh flaunts the body, God beautifies the spirit. I also want women to dress modestly, with decency and propriety, not with braided hair or gold or pearls or expensive clothes (1 Timothy 2:9, NIV).

2) A Godly Woman Always Seeks to be Holy in Her Conduct. Come, let's drink deep of love till morning; let's enjoy ourselves with love! My husband is not at home; he has gone on a long journey… (Proverbs 7:18 - 29, NIV)

A godly woman fears the Lord. She seeks God's will over the approval of anyone else on earth. Her fear of God makes her aware of the future consequence of her choices. A godly woman avoids any present situation that would be destructive for her future usefulness to God. Do you not know that your body is a temple of the Holy Spirit, who is in you, whom you have received from God? You are not your own; you were bought at a price. Therefore honor God with your body. (1 Corinthians 6:19-20, NIV)

3) A Godly Woman Always Seeks to be Truthful in Speech and Motives. With her enticing speech she caused him to yield, With her flattering lips she seduced him. Immediately he went after her, as an ox goes to the slaughter, Or as a fool to the correction of the stocks, Till an arrow struck his liver. As a bird hastens to the snare, He did not know it [would cost] his life. (Proverbs 7:21-23,NKJV)

This deceitful woman is an ugly woman because she is self-driven and wants her way. Her words and actions lead the man on a path to destruction. A beautiful woman wears heavenly beauty as God's Word describes it.

4) A Godly Woman Seeks to be Gentle and Quiet. The woman Folly is loud; she is undisciplined and without knowledge. (Proverbs 9:13, NIV) She is loud and defiant, her feet never stay at home (Proverbs 7:11 NIV)

This includes disrespect, hostility, aggressiveness and cunningness. All of these qualities are bad news.

And the Lord's servant must not quarrel; instead, he must be kind to everyone, able to teach, not resentful. (2 Timothy 2:24, NIV)

Instead, it should be that of your inner self, the unfading beauty of a gentle and quiet spirit, which is of great worth in God's sight. (1 Peter 3:4, NIV)

5_Wives, likewise, be submissive to your own husbands, that even if some do not obey the word, they, without a word, may be won by the conduct of their wives, when they observe your chaste conduct accompanied by fear. Do not let your adornment be merely outward—arranging the hair, wearing gold, or putting on fine apparel— rather let it be the hidden person of the heart, with the incorruptible beauty of a gentle and quiet spirit, which is very precious in the sight of God. For in this manner, in former times, the holy women who trusted in God also adorned themselves, being submissive to their own husbands, as Sarah obeyed Abraham, calling him lord, whose daughters you are if you do good and are not afraid with any terror. Husbands, likewise, dwell with them with understanding, giving honor to the wife, as to the weaker vessel, and as being heirs together of the grace of life, that your prayers may not be hindered. (1 Peter 3:1-7)11) A Godly Woman Seeks to Internalize Biblical Wisdom. She opens her mouth with wisdom, And on her tongue [is] the law of kindness. (Proverbs 31:26, NKJV). The Word is in her heart and life and so it comes out of her mouth. And when it does it is dressed in the clothes of the Spirit, gentle and kind.

# 7

# MOTHER AND SON RELATIONSHIP

The mother-son relationship is beautiful, and it enhances as the child grows. The son can never imagine his life without his mother, while the mother's affection and care for her son are eternal. However, with time, this relationship could experience certain changes. It doesn't mean that the son has stopped loving his mother, but the priorities may take a shift. Hence, they must hold on to each other come what may.

There are a lot of tips out there for a good mother/daughter relationship, but maintaining a healthy mother/son relationship is tricky and less talked about. Learn the keys to showing your son the ropes in life and staying connected as he grows.More:

1_Be Affectionate:

Parents tend to limit their affection for boys but shower girls with love and hugs. The term "mama's boy" leads us to believe that affection and attachment stunts boys' masculinity. But being a steady source of hugs and comfort for your child (beyond just the baby stage) is one of the best things you can offer as a parent.

Knowing that his home and his mother's arms are a safe haven builds up a boy's self-confidence. He will want more space as the teen years approach, but a hug a day goes a long way to show him you care and power him through hard times.

2_Teach Him Kindness and Respect

The world could use more gentlemen — and more kindness in general. Teaching children the old-school rules of politeness, kindness, and respect is no easy task in our busy yet increasingly informal lives. But showing your son from a young age how to use the magic words, mind his mother (and father), and hold the door (not just for women but for whomever is right behind him) will make him a stand-up, standout guy down the line. Model good behavior in your relationships with your children and your spouse. Also, teach your son to respect women by valuing them for their intelligence and personality, not their appearance and domestic skills.

3_Ditch the "Tough Guy" Stereotype

Many parents expect their sons of all ages to be Mr. Tough Guy with a "thicker skin" than girls. The fact is, it's healthy for boys and men to cry and show emotions like love, sadness, grief, and fear rather than bottle them up inside. There's no such thing as male emotions and female emotions — we're all human. Also, society leads us to believe that boys shouldn't play with dolls, play dress-up, take dance lessons, or participate in anything that isn't "rough and tumble." Allow your son to explore and enjoy all kinds of activities, just as you might with a daughter who's a "tomboy."

4_Discipline Him Wisely

Loose rules are not helpful for boys. Boys tend to be very literal and can't always read between the lines. They might push the limits if you don't set up firm but fair standards. At the same time, when disciplining your son, choose your words and punishments carefully. Keep in mind that spanking can result in aggression in kids later on, and name-calling and excessive yelling may cause emotional issues. Even when he gets on your last nerve, try to keep your cool and talk with him about what he's doing wrong and why you want him to stop. Take a break from each other when things get heated and return to the issue when everyone has calmed down. Be consistent in your expectations and consequences.

5_Don't Make Him the Man of the House

There are moms who do it all for their sons, and then there are mothers who expect their sons to do it all. If you're a single mom or your husband is working all the time, don't get confused about your son's role in your life. Sure, he should know how to do his fair share of chores and take on some financial responsibility in his teens. But his primary focus should be on his schooling and social development as a kid. Even if he's a mature, capable young man, don't unload your marital woes or your home maintenance to-do list on your son. If you put the weight of the world on his shoulders, he could come to resent you.


6_Plan Time for Play and Exploration

Boys benefit tremendously from playtime and exploration. Recent studies have linked children's recess and playtime with better focus and performance in school. Boys of all ages need to move their bodies and enjoy some healthy competition every day. Even though you're busy, block out some regular time for backyard games on sunny days, basement games on rainy days, as well as some unstructured play. The research shows that even just 15 minutes of playtime can help your child focus better on schoolwork. Playtime is also a great opportunity to connect with your child or teen.

7_Be Smart About Sports

Encouraging athleticism and being your kids' #1 fan is awesome. But some parents take cheering on their son to a whole new level. Resist becoming so entrenched in your child's sport that it turns into "your thing" or lowers your expectations for his grades and academics. Even if you're the sport's booster club president, don't push your son into sticking with it if he is failing in school or has a strong desire to quit. There's something to be said for committing to a sport or hobby through a season or trial period, but forcing a child to do something he doesn't like or that causes him to suffer in school can backfire.

8_Don't Play Favorites

Moms often develop a natural closeness with a particular child in their family. If it turns into favoritism, it can quickly lead to sibling rivalry. All kids are sensitive to favoritism, regardless of their sex or the sex of their siblings. Even when they push your buttons, try to handle all your children with fairness and care. Don't compare your children's grades, weight, sports performance, or anything that can be measured: it can be bad for sibling relations, and can be even worse for the parent/child bond

Here are a lot of tips out there for a good mother/daughter relationship, but maintaining a healthy mother/son relationship is tricky and less talked about. Learn the keys to showing your son the ropes in life and staying connected as he grows.More: 25 Quotes All Boy Moms Can Relate To

Be Affectionate

Parents tend to limit their affection for boys but shower girls with love and hugs. The term "mama's boy" leads us to believe that affection and attachment stunts boys' masculinity. But being a steady source of hugs and comfort for your child (beyond just the baby stage) is one of the best things you can offer as a parent. Knowing that his home and his mother's arms are a safe haven builds up a boy's self-confidence. He will want more space as the teen years approach, but a hug a day goes a long way to show him you care and power him through hard times.

Teach Him Kindness and Respect

The world could use more gentlemen — and more kindness in general. Teaching children the old-school rules of politeness, kindness, and respect is no easy task in our busy yet increasingly informal lives. But showing your son from a young age how to use the magic words, mind his mother (and father), and hold the door (not just for women but for whomever is right behind him) will make him a stand-up, standout guy down the line. Model good behavior in your relationships with your children and your spouse. Also, teach your son to respect women by valuing them for their intelligence and personality, not their appearance and domestic skills.

Ditch the "Tough Guy" Stereotype

Many parents expect their sons of all ages to be Mr. Tough Guy with a "thicker skin" than girls. The fact is, it's healthy for boys and men to cry and show emotions like love, sadness, grief, and fear rather than bottle them up inside. There's no such thing as male emotions and female emotions — we're all human. Also, society leads us to believe that boys shouldn't play with dolls, play dress-up, take dance lessons, or participate in anything that isn't "rough and tumble." Allow your son to explore and enjoy all kinds of activities, just as you might with a daughter who's a "tomboy."

Discipline Him Wisely

Loose rules are not helpful for boys. Boys tend to be very literal and can't always read between the lines. They might push the limits if you don't set up firm but fair standards. At the same time, when disciplining your son, choose your words and punishments carefully. Keep in mind that spanking can result in aggression in kids later on, and name-calling and excessive yelling may cause emotional issues. Even when he gets on your last nerve, try to keep your cool and talk with him about what he's doing wrong and why you want him to stop. Take a break from each other when things get heated and return to the issue when everyone has calmed down. Be consistent in your expectations and consequences.

Build His Life Skills

You used to change his every diaper and spoon-feed him every meal. As a mom, it's easy to fall into a pattern of doing it all for your children, even into their teen years — but that's not healthy for you or them. Just as you might do with a daughter, involve your son in cooking, cleaning, and a variety of household chores. Lacing life skills into his childhood will help lighten your load as a busy mom and set him up for independence after high school. (Bonus: His future spouse will thank you!)

Stay Involved in His Education

Boys are disproportionately affected by ADHD and retention in school. Early on, make sure to communicate regularly with his teacher, help him with homework, and address the disorganization problems many boys face. Getting your son more organized by his teen years will help him stay on track academically down the road.

Know When to Step In and When to Butt Out

As a mom, you manage a lot in your own life and your family's, so it's easy to get confused in your "Mama Bear" role and "fix" any problems or mistakes that arise. It's great that you want to protect your child, but try not to micromanage your son's life. If he gets a bad grade or has trouble with a teammate, talk with him about it first — don't pick up the phone to demand that his teacher change the grade or to report the problem to his coach. Pay attention to serious patterns — things like his grades dropping or his group of friends changing overnight — and talk with him about what's going on, what outcome he hopes for, and how you can support him. But remember that it's his life, and he'll learn a lot by rising to challenges himself.

Don't Make Him the Man of the House

There are moms who do it all for their sons, and then there are mothers who expect their sons to do it all. If you're a single mom or your husband is working all the time, don't get confused about your son's role in your life. Sure, he should know how to do his fair share of chores and take on some financial responsibility in his teens. But his primary focus should be on his schooling and social development as a kid. Even if he's a mature, capable young man, don't unload your marital woes or your home maintenance to-do list on your son. If you put the weight of the world on his shoulders, he could come to resent you.

Plan Time for Play and Exploration

Boys benefit tremendously from playtime and exploration. Recent studies have linked children's recess and playtime with better focus and performance in school. Boys of all ages need to move their bodies and enjoy some healthy competition every day. Even though you're busy, block out some regular time for backyard games on sunny days, basement games on rainy days, as well as some unstructured play. The research shows that even just 15 minutes of playtime can help your child focus better on schoolwork. Playtime is also a great opportunity to connect with your child or teen.

Be Smart About Sports

Encouraging athleticism and being your kids' #1 fan is awesome. But some parents take cheering on their son to a whole new level. Resist becoming so entrenched in your child's sport that it turns into "your thing" or lowers your expectations for his grades and academics. Even if you're the sport's booster club president, don't push your son into sticking with it if he is failing in school or has a strong desire to quit. There's something to be said for committing to a sport or hobby through a season or trial period, but forcing a child to do something he doesn't like or that causes him to suffer in school can backfire.

Don't Play Favorites

Moms often develop a natural closeness with a particular child in their family. If it turns into favoritism, it can quickly lead to sibling rivalry. All kids are sensitive to favoritism, regardless of their sex or the sex of their siblings. Even when they push your buttons, try to handle all your children with fairness and care. Don't compare your children's grades, weight, sports performance, or anything that can be measured: it can be bad for sibling relations, and can be even worse for the parent/child bond.

Remember Your Own Teen Years

The teen years can be frightening for any parent. Your son may start to pull away, becoming more independent, private, and defiant. He's starting to test the waters on his way to adulthood. This is a great time to tap into your memories of being a teen and try to be as understanding as possible. Think about what your own parents could have done better when you were a teen. Have the crucial discussions about drugs and alcohol and the birds and the bees with your son, but also give him space and offer him trust and room to grow. Work on communication during disagreements, and also keep in mind the

challenges he faces as a modern teenager who's finding his way. Good luck!.eenager who's finding his way. Good luck!.

# 8

# MOTHER AND DAUGHTER RELATIONSHIP

The relationship between a mother and daughter is special. A mother's love for her daughter cannot be described in words. Some things are hard to say, but it can be felt. The bond between a mother and daughter is strong, and the mother-daughter bonding can start at an early age. However, sometimes, the relation between a mother and her daughter may get a little complicated.

On some days, you might go shopping with your daughter and have fun or just sit with her at home and listen to her when she tells you about her big dreams and future plans, but there will also be days when your daughter would not listen to you or disobey you. At that time, you might feel that your relationship is falling apart, but deep down you'd know that your daughter loves you. Yes, in her teenage years she might behave a little strange, but she will come around. And it is during these years that you will have to work hard on your relationship.

Why is a Mother-Daughter Relationship Important?

The relationship that a girl shares with her mother can affect her sense of self-esteem, self-worth, sense of identity, and her ability to make friends. Children who are encouraged and praised (healthy praise, of course!) by their parents grow up to be confident individuals. If a child is not appreciated by her parents, she may seek validation from others.

When a girl is in her teenage years, she usually looks up to her mother. Her mother is her role model and she wishes to be like her. She gets her perfect image of a woman from her mother. But the relationship between a mother and daughter can go through many ups and downs. Many things can derail the harmonious relationship between a mother and her daughter. Temperaments, personality, experiences, hormones can all affect their relationship. Whatever may be the cause, it can be worked upon.

How to Build and Maintain a Strong Bond with Your Daughter

Here are some ways to help you improve your bond with your daughter:

1. When She is a Little Girl

It is important to forge a strong connection from the very start, i.e., soon after the birth of your daughter. Some things to keep in mind are as follows:

Breastfeed Your Daughter

By breastfeeding your little angel, you can develop a strong bond with her. The release of oxytocin hormone (the love hormone) during breastfeeding makes the mother fall in love with her baby even more, and this only helps in improving the bond between mother and daughter. Breastfeed your daughter in the first six months of her life. You can also enlist the help of a trained nurse to assist you with the task. Also, hold and cuddle your baby as much as possible to make her feel loved, comfortable, and safe. If you are unable to breastfeed your baby for some reason, try to maintain skin contact with her. Skin-to-skin contact between the mother and her child also strengthens the bond between the two.

Set a Routine

Spend some time with your daughter daily. Plan special weekend trips or getaways with your daughter. This will strengthen your bond. You can play dress up with your daughter, comb her hair, or brush her tooth while she is young – all these activities will bring you two closer. In case your daughter tries to imitate you, let her. Take it as an opportunity to model good behaviour. Also, encourage her to love her imperfections and try to find good in the negative things.

A mother and her daughter play dress up

Express Your Affection Openly

Express your affection to her openly If your daughter does something good, let her know that you are proud of her. This shows how much you love her. Nurture your bond with your daughter by sharing hugs, cuddles, and kisses. For example, you can incorporate extensive cuddle time during bedtime. These physical acts of love may teach your daughter to freely demonstrate and accept affection.

Share Your Experiences

The greatest gift you can give your daughter while she is young is your time. Take out time from your schedule to focus and spend some time with her to let her know that you value her as an individual. Make her feel special by sharing your joys and sorrows with her. Also, involve her in household chores from an early age to develop a sense of responsibility in her.

## 2. When She is a Teenager/Adult

When a girl is in her teenage years, it can be a difficult time for her. A daughter needs her mother the most in her teenage years and also when she gets married. Here is what you will need to remember when your daughter becomes a teenager:

Be There for Her

Adolescence can be a difficult phase for your girl because, at that time, she will try to find her identity and will struggle to cope up with the various physical and emotional changes she will go through. Make sure you provide her necessary guidance and support, and hear her out. Do offer her advice, but don't command her as she might become rebellious. Just listen to her concerns and try to channelise her stress or anger positively.

Respect Her Feelings

Honour your daughter's boundaries. As much as you may prefer to be with her, if she desires some 'alone time', give that to her. On some days, you might make mistakes too. Be a bigger person and own up to your mistakes. Simply apologise and make amends. Respect her individuality and allow her to explore her inner worth and interests without inhibition.

A mother with her teenage daughter

Talk to Her Freely

Talk to your daughter about various worldly issues. You can share your pearls of wisdom while going shopping with her or while cooking meals. As a teenager, she may feel insecure about her body. Help her accept and be proud of her body. Talk to her about relationships, character traits like faith, integrity, perseverance, and courage. Let her know that these are the values she will need the most in her life. Empower and equip her with all your wisdom and life experiences.

Keep Realistic Expectations

As parents, it is normal to have certain expectations from children. But it is important to be reasonable. Remember your daughter is a separate individual who may have her dreams and aspirations. Give her space to grow and blossom by giving ample support and love.

It is a mother who educates her daughters about different things. It is a mother who teaches her daughter how to handle and carry herself in this world and how to deal with different sets of people and sail through various walks of life. A mother is the first friend of her daughter, who guides her throughout lives. If you have a daughter, make sure you be there for her always and support her in all walks of life.

# 9

# WAYS TO FIX YOUR BROKEN RELATIONSHIP WITH YOUR CHILD

How can I repair this relationship?

Disrepair happens slowly. You may not even notice that it's happening at the time.

Then, one day, you realize how far you've drifted from one another.

It can feel shocking, sad, frustrating, or lonely.

But, you don't have to stay stuck in a distant relationship. There are things you can do to repair a relationship with your child, even if it feels like an impossible task.

Here are a few tips to get you started.

How to mend a broken relationship with your son or daughter.

Acknowledge the rift: In a calm moment, let your child know what you've observed and how you feel about it. Your child's response may vary. They may agree, disagree, be indifferent, angry or annoyed. Whatever their response, keep the focus on your own thoughts and feelings, rather than forcing them to agree or feel the same. "I realize things have been a little tense between us. That makes me sad, I want to work on easing that tension."

Make Amends: Rather than focusing on your child's behavior or actions, take responsibility for your part in the disrepair. Have you been busy, impatient, frustrated, controlling, etc? Apologize and work on making it right with your child. Keep it simple, and avoid adding"...but, you should..." to the end. "I'm sorry that I've been distracted after school lately, I'm going to put my phone away, so I can focus on listening better."

Engage in an activity together: Rather than allowing the distance to continue, work to find something to do that gives you a chance to be together. It may be a board game, shooting baskets, taking a walk or even playing a video game. Sometimes, it's best to just be together in silence, rather than forcing your child to talk. If your child is resistant, keep the door open and continue to look for opportunities to spend time together.

Do something different: Replace negative communication patterns with something helpful or positive. That may mean taking a deep breath before responding to your child, focusing on listening rather than giving advice or working on being empathetic (even if you don't necessarily agree). It may take time for this new behavior to become a habit. In the meantime give yourself permission to be a "work                              in                              progress."

# 10

## TOP TIPS ON HOW TO BE A GOOD MOTHER AND WIFE

Who is a good wife and mother?

She is that loving and caring woman who cares enough and seeks to know more about being perfect for her husband and children.

The question is:

Where do you belong?

A good mother, or a bad wife.

You alone can answer the question.

Don't be afraid my dear, nobody is perfect, but we only strive to be always.

And if you are reading this post now, that means you are looking for how to be a good mother and wife. Thankfully, you can be one if you follow my description.

The truth remains that if you are hoping to have a good man as your husband, your husband and the children also look for that good woman, the mother too.

If you want to be that good wife your husband wants, then you have to follow these 9 steps.

9 Characteristics of a Good Wife And Mother.

1) You Can't be perfect, So Stop Trying:-

There's no need to struggle every day to be the good woman in your picture because it can never be attained. No one is perfect, not even you.

2) Always be Happy:-

A Happy wife they said is a good wife. Happiness is contagious, which means that when you are happy, both your husband and the children become happy too and everything flows with it.

When you are not happy, probably you are lost in the thought of how to be the best wife and mum, which is not achievable, then you affect everyone else negatively.

The best way to be happy is to love yourself and the way you are, do everything you love to do that makes you happy, and then keep a positive attitude always.

Stop trying to live your life by the book, or live for anybody. Your happiness matters the most.

3) Be a worthy mother for your children:-

I found out that children are always so attached to their mother than their father: this is why you must become an ideal mum to them.

Be the mother they will depend on and confide in when they are challenged.

Another quality of a good mother and wife is the ability to raise respectful, honest, and loving children who have good values and respect for their parents and elders.

4) Learn To Always Have fun:-

Every day in marriage is not always rosy. Some days may be worse than the other. There are days you will ask yourself if you have made a mistake for getting married at all.

Those things can cause boredom. But you have to Remain focused and have fun, knowing that "When you worry, you cause double problems for yourself." So do not entertain dull moments.

Threat yourself with good things like- going on dates, cinema. Just enjoy every moment of your life.

5) Be An Honest Person:-

Honesty is the bedrock for a successful relationship. No marriages can last long without open communication and honesty.

To be a good wife, your husband must feel your truthfulness and honesty.

One thing is that it takes a great deal to be honest, but it also pays in marriage.

Being truthful won't always be easy. Sometimes your honesty might get in the way between your husband and you, it may even cause some fights too.

But dishonesty destroys a relationship completely and it may even cause divorce in the long run When it has depleted all the trust in your relationship.

6) Show Love To Him:-

That sounds dumb, isn't it? But if you want to be a good wife and mother, you've got to understand how to love your husband unconditionally.

Don't wait till he meets certain criteria. Don't also wait until he meets all your needs before you love him.

Just love him irrespective of whether he is meeting your criteria or expectation. According to the Bible, love covers a multitude of sins.

When you love him unconditionally, his mistakes wouldn't be many problems for you because you know that nobody is perfect.

Love will make you overlook so many flaws.

# Epilogue

48

Hope u enjoyed this book QUALITY WOMAN,for you to achieve all that was stated in this book ,you need to put all details entailed in this book into action and you will see yourself transforming into that great QUALITY WOMAN.

www.ingramcontent.com/pod-product-compliance
Lightning Source LLC
Chambersburg PA
CBHW060227170726
48004CB00004BA/1467